THE PRAYER SOLUTION

But thou, when thou prayest, enter into thy
closet, and when thou hast shut thy door,
pray to thy Father which is in secret;
and thy Father which seeth in secret
shall reward thee openly.
Mathew6:6

By
Franklin N. Abazie

The Prayer Solution

COPYRIGHT 2017 BY Franklin N Abazie
ISBN: 978-1-945-133-60-2

All right reserved. This book or any portion thereof may not be reproduced or used in any manner whatsoever without the express written permission of the publisher, except for the use of brief quotations in a book review. All Bible-quotes are from King James Version and others as noted.

Published by: F N ABAZIE PUBLISHING HOUSE---a.k.a, Empowerment Bookstore

That I may publish with the voice of thanksgiving and tell of all thy wondrous works. **Psalms26:7**

To order additional copies, wholesales or booking: Call the Church office (973-372-7518)
or Empowerment Bookstore Hotline 973-393-8518
Worship address:
343 Sanford Avenue Newark New Jersey 07106
Administrative Head Office address:
33 Schley Street Newark New Jersey 07112
Email:pastorfranknto@yahoo.com
Website www.fnabaziehealingministries.org

Publishing House: www.fnabaziepublishinghouse.org

This book is a production of F N Abazie Publishing House.
A publication Arms of Miracle of God Ministries 2017
First Edition

CONTENTS

THE MANDATE OF THE COMMISSION............iv

ARMS OF THE COMMISSION...............................v

INTRODUCTION…………………….....……viii

CHAPTER 1

1. How to persist in prayers 27

CHAPTER 2

2. How to engage in warfare Prayers.......................33

CHAPTER 3

3. Prayer of Salvation...64

CHAPTER 4

4. About the Author..72

THE MANDATE OF THE COMMISSION

"THE MOMENT IS DUE TO IMPACT YOUR WORLD THROUGH THE REVIVAL OF THE HEALING & MIRACLE MINISTRY OF JESUS CHRIST OF NAZARETH.

I AM SENDING YOU TO RESTORE HEALTH UNTO THEE AND I WILL HEAL THEE OF THY WOUNDS, SAID THE LORD OF HOST."

ARMS OF THE COMMISSION

1) F N Abazie Ministries-Miracle of God Ministries (Miracle Chapel Intl)

2) F N Abazie TV Ministries: Global Television Ministry Outreach.

3) F N Abazie Radio Ministries: Radio Broadcasting Outreach.

4) F N Abazie Publishing House: Book Publication.

5) F N Abazie Bible School: also called Word of Healing Bible School (W.O.H.B.S)

6) F N Abazie Evangelistic Ass: Miracle of God Ministries: Global Crusade

7) Empowerment Bookstore: Book distribution.

8) F N Abazie Helping Hands: Meeting the help of the needy world wide

9) F N Abazie Disaster Recovery Mission: Global Disaster Recovery.

10) F N Abazie Prison Ministry: Prison Ministry for all convicts "Second chance"

Some of our ministry arms are waiting the appointed time to commence

FAVOR CONFESSION

Father thank you for making me righteous and accepted through the blood of Jesus Christ. Because of that, I am blessed and highly favored by God. I am the subject of your affection. Your favor surrounds me as a shield, and the first thing that people see around me is your favored shield.

Thank you that I have favor with you and man today. All day long people go out of their way to bless me and help me. I have favor with everyone that I deal with today. Doors that were once closed are now opened for me. I receive preferential treatment, and I have special privileges, I am Gods favored child.

No good thing will he withhold from me. Because of Gods favor my enemies cannot triumph over my life. I have supernatural increase and promotion. I declare restoration to everything that the devil has stolen from my life. I have honor in the midst of my adversaries and an increase in assets, especially in real estate and expansion of territories.

Because I am highly favored by God, I experience great victories, supernatural turnarounds, and miraculous breakthrough in the midst of great impossibilities. I receive recognition, prominence, and honor. Petitions are granted to me even by ungodly authorities. Policies, rules, regulations, and laws are changed and reverse on my behalf.

I win battles that I don't even have to fight, because God fights them for me. This is the day, the set time and the designated moment for me to experience the free favor of God, that profusely and lavishly abound on my behalf in Jesus name.

Amen.

INTRODUCTION

"And he spake a parable unto them to this end, that men ought always to pray, and not to faint." **Luke18:1**

I may never get the opportunity to meet you in person, however, I am glad to meet you through the pages of this small book. Prayer solution is a book of reality. In this publication, you will be armed with techniques to engage the enemy in battle. Besides warfare prayers, you will also appreciate the admonishment in this book, concerning what we must do to make our prayers productive.

I believe there is another dimension of prayer that generate concreate result. This book is a manual to help anyone tap into that dimension of prayer that comes with an instant divine intervention. This book will help anyone struggling with their prayer life.

In my own opinion, prayer as a form of spiritual labor must be done diligently and meticulously.

"Epaphras, who is one of you, a servant of Christ, saluteth you, always labouring fervently for you in prayers, that ye may stand perfect and complete in all the will of God."
Colossian4:12.

This book of prayer that will help anyone to develop a prayer life. Besides a prayerful life, we must be practical with our heart desires. Life is practical and not mystical. After we bombard the kingdom of hell with powerful warfare prayers, we must do something positive with our hands.

It is written *"For even when we were with you, this we commanded you, that if any would not work, neither should he eat."*
2theo3:10

The act of being responsible is a simple way to define a Christian.

It is written *"Whatsoever thy hand findeth to do, do it with thy might; for there is no work, nor device, nor knowledge, nor wisdom, in the grave, whither thou goest."*
Eccl9:10

Nobody one is permitted to be idle in life especially after praying powerful prayer, like the once you will see in the pages ahead.. Unless we develop a powerful prayer life of faith, we will never have the victory. I pray the Lord will help your understanding to day. I urge you to neglect my grammar but pay attention to the context of the text.

Happy reading.

HIS DESTINY WAS THE CROSS....

HIS PURPOSE WAS LOVE.....

HIS REASON WAS YOU....

But thou, when thou prayest, enter into thy closet, and when thou hast shut thy door, pray to thy Father which is in secret; and thy Father which seeth in secret shall reward thee openly.

Mathew6:7

WHY DON'T WE PRAY?

~Laziness

Most of us do not pray because we are lazy for the most part, more especially we do not pray because we have neglected the power of God in prayer. Please do not misunderstand me, great teaching is good, powerful preaching is awesome.

But the power of divine intervention is hidden in prayer. Studies have proven that the average Christian spends less than ten minutes per day in prayer. We are commanded to pray and not cease. Jesus said men ought to pray.

Although you may not be aware of it, but prayerlessness is a sin according to the holy bible. Every time we do not pray we sin against our God. But I am trusting the Father and believing that after you finish reading this book, you will pray unto God.

~Unbelieve

Unbelief will hinder anyone from developing a prayer life. Most of us claim we believe in God. But our corresponding action is the opposite.

The reason we don't pray is because we do not belief in our prayer to God.

The Bible says, *"He that cometh to God must believe that He is, and that He is a rewarder of them that diligently seek Him."* **(Hebrews 11:6).**

If you claim you are a believer then I urge you to develop a prayer life in Jesus Mighty Name.

It is written *"And in that day ye shall ask me nothing. Verily, verily, I say unto you, Whatsoever ye shall ask the Father in my name, he will give it you. Hitherto have ye asked nothing in my name: ask, and ye shall receive, that your joy may be full.*

John16:23-24.

~We Lack the Spiritual Discipline

As Holy and righteous as you may appear without spiritual discipline your spiritual fire will quench. For unless we develop ourselves in prayer we will never be able to accomplish any task in life.

It is written *"He that hath my commandments, and keepeth them, he it is that loveth me: and he that loveth me shall be loved of my Father, and I will love him, and will manifest myself to him."* **John14:21.**

And what is some of these commandment?

It written *"Watch and pray, that ye enter not into temptation: the spirit indeed is willing, but the flesh is weak."* **Mathew26:41.**

For unless we give ourselves whole to prayer and fasting we will ever remain baby Christians in life.

Remember...

"Delight thyself also in the Lord: and he shall give thee the desires of thine heart." **Psalms37:4.**

Anyone who is sold out to God is sold out to prayer. For unless we delight ourselves in prayer, we will never prevail with answer.

We must respect God and resolve it in our heart that nothing will get in our way of spending time with God.

We must set a specific time for daily prayer. It takes dedication and devotion to maintain a constant prayer life.

~We misplace our priorities

In my opinion, for unless we totally surrender our plans and purposes in life, we will never make praying a priority in life.

~There is sin in our Life

Unless we deal with sin in our lives, we can never be able to pray righteously.

~We Lack the Spirit of Prayer

There is a spirit of prayer. For most of us that pray we recognize the spirit of prayer. For unless we develop such spirit in our individual lives, prayer will forever be frustrating for anyone.

SOLUTION PRAYER POINTS

My Father, I am in your presence, avenge me of my adversaries, in Jesus Name.

Every power of domestic witchcraft, I destroy you in the Almighty Name of Jesus Name.

Strong man spirit from my father's house, I destroy you in the mighty Name of Jesus

By the blood of Jesus I destroy every hindering spirit militating against my rising in the Name of Jesus.

Father God Arise Judge my enemies your by fire in Jesus Name.

Let every garment of darkness on my body, CATCH FIRE! in Jesus Name.

Let every garment of shame, be roasted in the fire of Jesus

Every delay upon my life, receive the speed of God in Jesus Name.

I break every chain binding my finances, in Jesus Name.

By the blood of Jesus, I nullify every power of darkness, in Jesus Name.

Destiny snatcher, the blood of Jesus Christ is against you.

Father God arise, demonstrate your power by the blood of Jesus Christ.

Any power prolonging infirmity, DIE! in Jesus Name.

Arrows of infirmity assigned against my head, catch fire in Jesus Name.

Every plot of the enemy to silent my voice, I slay you in the spirit by the blood of Jesus.

Every arrow of the wicked against me back fire in Jesus Mighty Name

I destroy every power delegated against my future in the name of Jesus.

Every power causing frustration upon my life, I destroy you in the Nmae of Jesus.

Every enemy of my promotion I destroy you in the Name of Jesus.

Every operation of darkness in my family line, DIE! in Jesus Name

I recover ten-fold all my wasted years, in Jesus Name.

Mountain of affliction before me, I destroy you in the Name of Jesus.

Every dream affliction, Die! in Jesus Name.

This year, men shall compete to favour me, in Jesus Name.

Every evil hand that shall point to my star this year, W-H-I-T-H-E-R! in Jesus Name.

Every satanic malpractice over my family, I cut you off! in Jesus Name.

Every power assigned against my life be destropyed in Jesus Name

Every tongue speaking against my life, be destroyed in Jesus Name

Every power declaring that it is over for me, be crushed in Jesus Name

Every good thing that I have laid my hands upon, my hands shall finish it, in Jesus Name.

Every yoke upon my hands, B-R-E-A-K! in Jesus Name.

Any curse issued against my hands, B-R-E-A-K! in Jesus Name.

Thou power of bad luck, DIE! in Jesus Name.

Serpents of death; serpents of wastage, assigned against my hands, DIE! in Jesus Name.

My hands shall bury bad things; it shall not bury good things, in Jesus Name.

Any power that has tied down my destiny, BREAK-LOOSE, from my life, in Jesus Name.

Wherever the stars have been programmed to disturb my destiny, O God Arise! Manifest your POWER! in Jesus Name.

Every witchcraft power toying with my destiny, DIE! in Jesus Name.

O God of Elijah! ATTACK my red sea! in Jesus Name.

My Father! If I have been disconnected from the socket of my destiny, reconnect me by fire! in Jesus Name.

My Father, whatever you have not positioned into my life, wipe them off! in Jesus Name.

O God Arise! And dismantle the poison in my foundation! in Jesus Name.

Negative circumstances that is affecting my success, BOW! in Jesus Name.

I curse the spirit of backwardness, in Jesus Name.

Every witchcraft register bearing my destiny, C-A-T-C-H-F-I-R-E! in Jesus Name.

Every power delaying the manifestation of my breakthroughs, DIE! in Jesus Name.

O God Arise! And rearrange my circumstances to bring me into glory! in Jesus Name.

Every proclamation of the powers of darkness against my life, DIE! in Jesus Name.

O God Arise! And package testimonies for me in Jesus Name.

Satanic decree working against my life, DIE! in Jesus Name. (Nullify the decree, cancel it).

Every calendar of the enemy, working against my life, CLEAR AWAY! in Jesus Name.

You evil programmers, let me go! in Jesus Name.

Anything programmed into my foundation to waste my destiny, DIE! in Jesus Name.

You altar of evil programmers, assigned against my life, DIE! in Jesus Name.

My Father! If I have obeyed any evil command, KILL IT! in the name of Jesus.

Witchcraft programming; You are A LIAR! DIE! in the name of Jesus.

Any negative power, programmed against my head, JUMP OUT NOW! in the name of Jesus.

Satanic programming in the dream, Your Time Is Up! Therefore, DIE! in the name of Jesus.

Every witchcraft material planted into my life from the womb, DIE! in the name of Jesus.

My Father, whatever you have not positioned into my life, wipe them off! in Jesus Name.

O God Arise! And dismantle the poison in my foundation! in Jesus Name.

Negative circumstances that is affecting my success, BOW! in Jesus Name.

I curse the spirit of backwardness, in Jesus Name.

Every witchcraft register bearing my destiny, C-A-T-C-H-F-I-R-E! in Jesus Name.

Every power delaying the manifestation of my breakthroughs, DIE! in Jesus Name.

O God Arise! And rearrange my circumstances to bring me into glory! in Jesus Name.

Every proclamation of the powers of darkness against my life, DIE! in Jesus Name.

O God Arise! And package testimonies for me in Jesus Name.

Satanic decree working against my life, DIE! in Jesus Name. (Nullify the decree, cancel it).

In the Name of the King of kings, In the name of the Lord of lords, In the name of the President of presidents: JESUS CHRIST! Every witchcraft bondage in my life, B-R-E-A-K!

Any power calling my name into a cauldron, You Are A LIAR! DIE! in the name of Jesus.

Blood of Jesus, WIPE OFF every witchcraft name assigned against me, in the name of Jesus.

Every mouth of the wicked speaking against me, shut up in the name of Jesus.

Ministry of fear in my life, DIE! in the name of Jesus.

Every power stealing my promotion, DIE! in the name of Jesus.

Every abnormal pattern in my family line, DIE! in the name of Jesus. [Pray this seven hot times]

O God Arise and make me a wonder! in the name of Jesus.

Every power reporting me to witchcraft meetings, DIE! in the name of Jesus.

Every meeting summoned to waste my life, in the name of Jesus.

Every inherited power assigned to waste my destiny, come out now in the name of Jesus.

My wealth, buried in the earth, come forth in the name of Jesus.

Every arrow of witchcraft fired into my prosperity, DIE! in the name of Jesus.

You financial killer of my father's house, I am not your candidate! Therefore, DIE!! in the name of Jesus.

Expected and unexpected financial breakthrough, locate me by fire in the name of Jesus.

Poverty activator dreams, Hear the word of the Lord! Be destroyed in the name of Jesus.

O God Arise and use me to change my family history, in the name of Jesus.

My end shall be better than my beginning, in the name of Jesus.

Anything buried that is pulling me down, DIE! in the name of Jesus.

Oracles of my father's house, speaking against my progress, in the name of Jesus.

I rewrite my family history by the power in the blood of Jesus.

Any problem that came into my life through any dead relative, you are a liar, DIE!!! in the name of Jesus.

My life, reject wastage, in the name of Jesus.

Every agenda of the enemy to capture my spirit-man, FAIL! in the name of Jesus.

CHAPTER 1
HOW TO PERSIST IN PRAYERS

In my own opinion, it takes personal discipline to develop effective and efficient prayer life. For our prayers to be effective and efficient there is something critical and unique we must do. Every one desire to pray effectively but how many of us truly want to do what it takes for our prayer to generate result.

It is written *"And as he prayed, the fashion of his countenance was altered, and his raiment was white and glistering."* **Luke9:29.**

If Jesus pray until the fashion of his countenance was altered, so we ought to do the same to get the same result. For our prayers to generate result we must do the following; pray in faith, be devoted, be determined, be focused, be disciplined, and be humble in life.

Remember…..

"And he said unto them, Look on me, and do likewise: and, behold, when I come to the outside of the camp, it shall be that, as I do, so shall ye do." **Judges7:17.**

If you must persist in pray, then you must be devoted, disciplined, dedicated, focused, and have faith in God.

What are the secrets to having an effective prayer life?

~Persistent

There are so many biblical characters who persisted and prevailed in prayers during their days. Persistence in prayer literally means praying until something happens. It is the act of continual to prayer unto God, consistently day and night.

Regrettable most today church folks do not pray consistently. Most of us are not dedicated and devoted to prayer. For the most part God has done His part concerning our lives.

Chapter 1 - How to Persist in Prayers

We must wake up and pray unto God day and night if we must see our community and cities changed and transformed.

WHEN MUST I PERSIST IN PRAYER?

There is no time frame on when to persist in prayer especially if you are a Christian. We must persist in faith and in prayer daily. It takes a committed heart to persist before God in prayer.

In my opinion, just about any dummy can persist in prayer. For anyone to persist in prayer we must be determined, disciplined, devoted and be practical in life.

Every effective prayer must come from the heart. Until we are ready to pray from the heart, we deceive ourselves. Jesus warned us carefully in Mathew chapter six verses five.

"And when thou prayest, thou shalt not be as the hypocrites are: for they love to pray standing in the synagogues and in the corners of the streets, that they may be seen of men. Verily I say unto you, They have their reward."
Mathew6:5

".....The heartfelt and persistent prayer of a righteous man (believer) can accomplish much [when put into action and made effective by God—it is dynamic and can have tremendous power." **James 5:16**

What is Prayer?

Prayer is simply a devoted channel to talk to God, through an established two way communication channel. That is you speak, meditate, and wait for what God will say to you.

It is written *"I will stand upon my watch, and set me upon the tower, and will watch to see what he will say unto me, and what I shall answer when I am reproved."* **Habakkuk2:1**

How do I persist in prayers?

~ We must engage our heart in prayer

In my own opinion, prayer is a warfare. *"Unless we travail in prayers, we will not prevail with answers in life."* **--Franklin N Abazie.**

Chapter 1 - How to Persist in Prayers

"Unless we engage our heart in prayers, we will not persist or last in prayer. Hannah poured her soul unto the Lord and God remembered her and she received Samuel. Her mouth was not moving but her heart was fully engaged."

1 Samuel 1:13-19.

~ We must depend on the Holy Spirit

Unless we depend on the Holy Spirit we will not persist for a long time. As long as you pray from your flesh nature, you will not last. "if you do not fast , you will not last."

For fasting must be unto God and not after man. We must consciously depend on the Holy Spirit in prayer if we must prevail in life.

~We must engage in a cry of faith

It is a cry of faith in prayers that will secure heaven attention for us. For unless we pray and cry unto God in faith, we will not prevail not persist. Blind Bartimaeus persisted by crying out to Jesus-nonstop.

It is written *"When I cry unto thee, then shall mine enemies turn back: this I know; for God is for me."* **Psalm 56:9**

~We must engage effectual fervency in prayer

"We must build up our prayer life, and keep the fire burning from our spirit man. It is the intensity of our prayers that will help our persistence if we must prevails in prayer. Elijah prayed with fervency and the heaven obeyed his instructions. Rain did not fall for three and half years as he prayed and fell only after he prayed for rain to fall" **(James 5:16-18)**

~We must pray with a right motive from a be righteous heart.

Righteousness is an essential instrument if we must persist in prayers. For our righteousness to appear before God our motive must be pure and right before God. God will not allow anyone to persist with the wrong motive.

It is written *"Ye ask, and receive not, because ye ask amiss, that ye may consume it upon your lusts."* **James 4:3**

CHAPTER 2

HOW TO ENGAGE THE ENEMY IN WARFARE

"What is warfare prayer?"

Warfare prayer is a prayer strategy common with most charismatic and Christian faith denominations. It engages prayer as a weapon of warfare against the forces of evil. The truth is there are evil forces that hinders us (believers) in life.

Although, most practiced warfare prayer techniques are unbiblical these days, we must all be conscious not to be led astray by any seducing doctrine. Often promoters of warfare prayer often recommend praying prayers written by others—and to pray them repeatedly.

This practice in my opinion is not strategic and biblical. It is written *"For we wrestle not against flesh and blood, but against principalities, against powers, against the rulers of the darkness of this world, against spiritual wickedness in high places."* **Ephesians 6:12**

A few of some common techniques of the devil is to dominates, intimidates, and establish controls.

It is written *"For though we walk in the flesh, we do not war after the flesh: (For the weapons of our warfare are not carnal, but mighty through God to the pulling down of strong holds;) Casting down imaginations, and every high thing that exalteth itself against the knowledge of God, and bringing into captivity every thought to the obedience of Christ;"* **2cor10:3-5**

Every believer must recognized the presence of the Holy Spirit, develop faith, boldness, and authority. As spiritual law enforcement officers it is our duty to engage in warfare battles prayer against any demonic installation or any forces of hell.

How to Resist Sin and Temptation

For anyone to resist sin and temptation in life, we must learn to submit to God. It is written; *"Submit yourselves therefore to God. Resist the devil, and he will flee from you."* **James4:7**

Chapter 2 - How to Engage the Enemy in Warfare

Resist Carnal nature

Often our carnal man wants to delegate and be in charge. For unless we are spiritually minded we will lose the battle against the enemy.

It is written *"For to be carnally minded is death; but to be spiritually minded is life and peace. Because the carnal mind is enmity against God: for it is not subject to the law of God, neither indeed can be."* **Romans 8:6-7**

We must depend on the power of the Holy Spirit.

For unless we take advantage of the presence of the Holy Spirit, the enemy will deal with us severely.

It written *"For we wrestle not against flesh and blood, but against principalities, against powers, against the rulers of the darkness of this world, against spiritual wickedness in high places."* **Ephesians 6:12.**

Flee temptation.

Whenever we are tempted, the bible say that we are not being tempted by God but by our own lust.

It is written *"But every man is tempted, when he is drawn away of his own lust, and enticed. Then when lust hath conceived, it bringeth forth sin: and sin, when it is finished, bringeth forth death."* **James1:14-15**

We must not only run or walk away from temptation but flee from it. When Joseph was tempted by Potiphar's wife, he knew if he stayed he would give in to her advances.

"And she caught him by his garment, saying, Lie with me: and he left his garment in her hand, and fled, and got him out." **Gensis39:12**

We must present our body as a vessels of honor

Jesus is looking for a vessel of honor to use for the Kingdom of God.

Chapter 2 - How to Engage the Enemy in Warfare

For unless we present our body as vessel of honor for the master's use, the devil will defile use with sin.

It is written *"If a man therefore purge himself from these, he shall be a vessel unto honour, sanctified, and meet for the master's use, and prepared unto every good work. Flee also youthful lusts: but follow righteousness, faith, charity, peace, with them that call on the Lord out of a pure heart."*

2tim2:21-22

We must constantly confess and apply the word of God.

"Unless we all know and confess what is written, we will be written off."

Knowing the word of God, is knowing the will of God, and knowing His will is actualizing his plan and purpose for our lives.

PRAYER POINTS TO DEFEAT HOUSEHOLD WITCHCRAFT

I plead the blood of over my family in the name of Jesus.

I reject every arrow of carnality in my prayer life, in the name of Jesus.

Arise oh Lord and scatter my enemies, in the name of Jesus.

Let every witchcraft covens melt away like fire, in the name of Jesus.

Father God, visit all witchcraft plantation in my life in the name of Jesus.

O God cause confusion in witchcraft camps assigned against me, in the name of Jesus.

O earth reject to carry out any instruction of witchdoctors assigned against me in the name of Jesus.

I deprogram and cancel all witchcraft prophecies by the power in the blood of Jesus, in the name of Jesus.

Chapter 2 - How to Engage the Enemy in Warfare

I program judgment on witchcraft into the heavens, in the name of Jesus.

O God arise and cast abominable things upon witchcraft, in the name of Jesus.

My father let the table of witchcraft becomes their snare, in the name of Jesus.

Let human blood become a snare unto them in the name of Jesus.

Let the eyes of the witches assigned against me be darkened, in the name of Jesus.

Let their covens become desolate so that none can dwell in them, in the name of Jesus.

Pray this prayer three hot times: Let every witchcraft powers flying against me crash land and die, in the name of Jesus.

No witch or wizard shall prosper in my environment in the name of Jesus.

Water spirits that are networking with witchcraft against me, I judge you by fire, in the name of Jesus.

Queen of heaven that is networking with witchcraft against me, I judge you by fire, in the name of Jesus.

Let the sun go down on witchcraft powers, in the name of Jesus.

Let their days be dark in the name of Jesus.

Let the sun smite them by day and the moon by night, in the name of Jesus.

Let the stars in their curses fight against witches and wizards in the name of Jesus.

I shut down all witchcraft buildings with the key of David, in the name of Jesus.

O God arise and send out your whirlwind with great pain upon the head of witchcraft, in the name of Jesus.

O God arise and trample down every witchcraft coven in the name of Jesus.

O God arise and cause stormy wind to fall upon witchcraft powers in the name of Jesus.

Chapter 2 - How to Engage the Enemy in Warfare

O God arise and bring the day of disaster upon the heads of witchcraft in the name of Jesus.

Every spell and enchantment of witchcraft clear off in the name of Jesus.

Every agenda of witchcraft over my family I cut you off in the name of Jesus.

Witchcraft in the waters I crush you powers in the name of Jesus.

Witchcraft agenda for my destiny, I destroy you in the name of Jesus.

Every witchcraft power assigned to convert my life to a dustbin I dislodge you in the name of Jesus.

Witchcraft powers assigned to resurrect affliction in my life, die by fire in the name of Jesus.

Every witchcraft game plan over my success I destroy you, in the name of Jesus.

Every yoke manufactured by witchcraft to attack my life catch your owner in the name of Jesus.

Every pregnancy of sorrow assigned against my breakthrough by witchcraft powers I abort you now in the name of Jesus.

I offset every witchcraft plan set up against my life, in the name of Jesus.

I break every witchcraft imprisonment over my life in the name of Jesus.

Every witchcraft remote control against my life I block you out in the name of Jesus.

Witchcraft powers sponsoring repeated problems in my life carry your problems in the name of Jesus.

I speak destruction unto every occultist assigned against me, in the name of Jesus.

Every household witchcraft assigned to waste my life be wasted in the name of Jesus.

Chapter 2 - How to Engage the Enemy in Warfare

Witchcraft altars and priests, die in the name of Jesus.

Every yoke designed by marine powers against my life, break in the name of Jesus.

Every evil load of witchcraft go back to your sender in the name of Jesus.

Every witchcraft prayer against my life scatter, in the name of Jesus.

Every environmental witchcraft be disgraced in the name of Jesus.

Witchcraft grip upon my family be dismantled in the name of Jesus.

Witchcraft initiations melt by fire in the name of Jesus.

Satanic decree over my life I cancel you now in the name of Jesus.

Witchcraft manipulations of my finances die in the name of Jesus.

Every witchcraft padlock hanging against me lock your owner in the name of Jesus.

Every witchcraft engagement over my success break in the name of Jesus.

Every ancestral witchcraft claim over my life break in the name of Jesus.

I destroy the power of stagnation and limitation in the name of Jesus.

I cut down every tree of failure in my family line, in the name of Jesus.

I destroy every pin of witchcraft in my family line, in the name of Jesus.

Every witchcraft covenant working against my life be broken in Jesus name.

Every witchcraft register bearing my name catch fire in the name of Jesus.

Every witchcraft documents written against me be consumed by fire, in the name of Jesus.

Every witchcraft informant that is observing my destiny be paralyzed, in the name of Jesus.

Chapter 2 - How to Engage the Enemy in Warfare

Every image carved against me catch fire, in the name of Jesus.

Every witchcraft authority over my destiny break in the name of Jesus.

Every tree planted against my freedom catch fire in the name of Jesus.

Every satanic road block clear away by fire in the name of Jesus.

Every witchcraft concoction inside my body melt away by fire in the name of Jesus.

I clear off every Beelzebub web over my life, in the name of Jesus.

My father arise in your anger and pursues my pursuer, in the name of Jesus.

Every foundation of witchcraft in my family catch fire, in the name of Jesus.

Father God destroy all assigned agents against my life in the Nme of Jesus.

Every seat of witchcraft working against me receive the fire of God in the name of Jesus.

Let their communication system be disrupted and be destroyed in the name of Jesus.

Let their throne be dismantled by fire and by thunder of God in the name of Jesus.

Fire of God destroy any opposition against my life in the name of Jesus.

Let the east wind of God pull down the strong hold of stubborn witchcraft in the name of Jesus.

I disintegrate and scatter all the network of witchcraft in the name of Jesus.

Let the transportation of witchcraft power catch fire and burn to ashes in the name of Jesus.

Every intermediaries and agents of witchcraft in my family receive double confusion in the name of Jesus.

Let the weapons of the enemy turn against them in the name of Jesus.

Chapter 2 - How to Engage the Enemy in Warfare

I speak confusion into the storehouses of witchcraft and I enter in and possess my possession in the name of Jesus.

Let their altars catch fire and burn to ashes in the name of Jesus.

I use the hammer of God to destroy their padlock in the name of Jesus.

Let the traps, nets and snares of the enemy catch them unawares in the name of Jesus.

Every astral projection undertaken by the enemies for my sake backfire in the name of Jesus.

Every witchcraft burial of my destiny receive fire and be exhumed in the name of Jesus.

Every bewitchment of my life receive the Holy Ghost fire in the name of Jesus.

Raise your right hand to the heavenlies and shout this out loud and clear: The blood of Jesus, Holy Ghost fire fall upon my hands in the name of Jesus. Lay the hand on your head now and pray like this: Identification mark of witchcraft hear the word of the Lord backfire in the name of Jesus.

Any power summoning my spirit man to witchcraft coven fall down and die, in the name of Jesus.

My father expose the human beings that are working with satan to trouble my life in the name of Jesus.

Any powers drawing my blood vomit it and die in the name of Jesus.

Every power that has tasted my blood will not stop vomiting until it confesses in the name of Jesus.

Blood of Jesus cause confusion in the stomach of witchcraft in the name of Jesus.

Thou power of witchcraft monitor die in the name of Jesus.

Chapter 2 - How to Engage the Enemy in Warfare

It is written there will be no peace for witchcraft because the bible says there is no peace for the wicked in the name of Jesus.

Automatic spiritual cage break in the name of Jesus.

Let the night birds of witchcraft be massacred by the angels of God in the name of Jesus.

Street junction witchcraft militating against my life die in the name of Jesus.

Witchcraft from my place of birth militating against my life die in the name of Jesus.

Every witchcraft poison be destroyed in the name of Jesus.

I overthrow any kingdom of witchcraft assigned against my life in the name of Jesus.

Blood of Jesus block the flying route of witchcraft assigned against me in the name of Jesus.

Every witchcraft exchange of my virtues be frustrated in the name of Jesus.

Every witchcraft pot cooking my destiny I bring the judgement of God against you in the name of Jesus.

Local and international witchcraft assigned against my life scatter in the name of Jesus.

Wisdom of household wickedness be converted to foolishness in the name of Jesus.

Let the wickedness of witchcraft power overtake them by the power in the blood of Jesus, in the name of Jesus.

Any witchcraft power projecting into the body of an animal in order to do me harm be trapped in that body forever, in the name of Jesus.

Let every witchcraft power be covered with shame in the name of Jesus.

Every chain of inherited witchcraft in my family break in the name of Jesus.

Every wisdom of witchcraft working against me be converted to madness in the name of Jesus.

Chapter 2 - How to Engage the Enemy in Warfare

Let the imagination of witchcraft against me be neutralized in the name of Jesus.

Every witchcraft decision against my life be scattered in the name of Jesus.

O God smites witchcraft powers by their cheekbones in the name of Jesus.

Every witchcraft burial of my virtues I reverse you now in the name of Jesus.

Any tongue anointed by satan against me catch fire in the name of Jesus.

Witchcraft powers assigned against my heavens scatter in the name of Jesus.

CONCLUSION

"Call unto me, and I will answer thee, and show thee great and mighty things, which thou knowest not." **Jer33:3**

This small book will still not make sense to you if you have not confess Jesus as your Lord and savior. No matter how far you have gone in the wrong direction, you will never get to your destination. I like to take a minute and ask you a sincere question here. Have you given your life to Jesus?

We were told *"Therefore if any man be in Christ, he is a new creature: old things are passed away; behold, all things are become new."* **2cor5:17**

What must I do to determine my divine visitation?

To determine divine visitation you must be born again! The word says as many as received him, to them gave He power to become the sons of God. Even to them that believe on his name.

Chapter 2 - How to Engage the Enemy in Warfare

To qualify for divine visitation do the following sincerely,

1) Acknowledge that you are a sinner and that He died for you. **Rom3:23.**

2) Repent of your sins. **Acts 3:19, Luke13:5, 2Peter3:9**

3) Believe in your heart that Jesus died for your sin. **Romans10:10**

4) Confess Jesus as the Lord over your life. **Romans10:10, Acts2:21**

Now repeat this Prayer after me

Say Lord Jesus, I accept you today, as my Lord and my savior, forgive me of my sins wash me with your blood. Right now, I believe, I am sanctified, I am save, I am free, I am free from the Power of sin to serve the Lord Jesus. Thank you Lord for saving me. Amen.

Congratulations: YOU ARE NOW A BORN AGAIN CHRISTIAN

Watch as the Spirit of God bears witness with our Spirit confirming His word with signs following.

The word says The Spirit itself beareth witness with our spirit, that we are the children of God.

Join a bible believing church or join us on our weekly and Sunday worship services at 343 Sanford Avenue Newark New Jersey 07106.

WISDOM KEYS

Every Productive Society is a society heading to the top

Millions of Nigerians run away from Nigeria, very few Nigerians stay in Nigeria.

My decision to return Nigeria is the will of God for my life

My short coming in America after 18 years, trained me to be wise, to think, reflect and reason appropriately.

Chapter 2 - How to Engage the Enemy in Warfare

If you train your mind to reason it will train your hands to earn money.

It is absurd to use the money of the heathen to build the kingdom of the living God.

Every Ministry reveals its agenda and goal either at the beginning or at the end. Be careful of your life it is your first Ministry.

The average American mind is conditioned for a continual quest to get new things and (discard the former) and throw away old things.

When I considered well, my BMW jeep became my initial deposit for the work of the ministry in Nigeria

Everyone is waiting for you to change your mind until you change your thinking nothing changes around you.

Multiple academic degrees in other discipline gave me the chance to think, reflect and reason

What so everyone are thinking and reflecting at the moment reveals you to the time and the now factor

All events and intents are the product of precise thought processes, accurate reason every event is designed for a designated timeline

Wisdom is your ability to think, to create and invent. If you can think wise enough you will come out of penury

The distance between you and success is your creative ability to think reason and reflect accurate.

Success is the result of hard work, commitment resolve and determination learning from past mistakes and failing.

If you organize your mind you have organized your life and destiny.

There is a thin line between success and failure. If you look above and beyond you are on your way to success.

Wealth is your ability to think, power is your ability to reason and success is your ability to be informed.

Chapter 2 - How to Engage the Enemy in Warfare

If you can make use of your mind by thinking and reasoning God will make use of your life and destiny.

Think and Be Great

Reflect, Reason, think and be great

Famous people are born of woman

That you will make it is your intention; that you will survive is your resolve, that you will succeed with changes is your determination, personal efforts and hard work.

No man was born a failure. Lack of vision is the end product of failure.

Working with mental patients encourages and aspire me to be a productive observant and dedicated to my assignment.

Successful people are not magicians, it is the will power combined with hard work, and determination and a resolve to succeed that make them succeed.

In the unequivocal state of the mind, intention is not a location or a position it is the state of the mind.

So many people think that they think. The mind is used to think reflect and reason. You will remain blind with your eye open until you can see with your mind by thinking.

There is no favoritism in accurate and precise calculation

Although knowledge is power, information is the key and gateway to a great future.

It will take the hand of God to move the hand of man.

With the backing of the great wise God, nothing will disconnect you from your inheritance.

As long as you have wisdom and understanding of God, Satan and evil cannot manipulate your life and destiny.

You have come this far by yourself judgment and decision you have made in the past, now lean and listen to God for another dimension of greatness.

Chapter 2 - How to Engage the Enemy in Warfare

Great people are common people it is extra ordinary effort and the price of sacrifice that produces greatness.

As a mental direct care worker I saw a great pastor and a motivational speaker within myself.

Menial job does not reduce your self-worth, until you resolve to achieve greatness see greatness in all you do; you will never count in your community.

The principle of Jesus will solve your gambling and addiction problems

The man of Jesus will lead you into heaven,

Everyone have their self-appraisal and what they think about you. Until you discover yourself other opinion about you will alter the real you.

Supervisors and directors are just a position in the chain of command in a work place. Never allow your supervisor hierarchy to alter your opinion about yourself.

Everyone can come out of debt if they make up their mind.

That I am not a decision maker at work does not diminish my contribution to my world.

Although it appears like it was a poor decision to accept a direct care employment at a psychiatric hospital as I reflect of my nine years of experience, it became apparent that I have learnt and experienced enough for my next assignment.

Self-encouragement and determination is a resolve of the heart.

If you are determined to make a difference, and do the things that make a difference you will eventually make a difference.

Good things do not come easy

Short cuts will cut your life short.

Those who look ahead move ahead.

Life is all about making an impact. In your life time strive to make an impact in your community.

Make friends and connect with people who are moving ahead of you in life.

Chapter 2 - How to Engage the Enemy in Warfare

If you can look around well you have come a long way in your life, made a lot of difference and realized a lot of success in life.

If you are my old friend, hurry up to reach out to me before I become a stranger to you.

Everything I am blessed with inspirations from God, that change my definition and interpretation of the world around me.

I thought I was stagnant and lonely until I looked around and noticed my children running around and my wife cooking.

At 40 I resigned my Job to seek the Lord forever.

My ministry took a drastic rise to the top when the wisdom of God visited me with knowledge and understanding.

You will be a better person if you understand the characteristics of your personality – your mood swings attitudes and habits.

It is the seed of love you sow into the heart of a child and a woman that you reap in due time.

Love is not selfish, love share everything including the concealed secrets of the mind.

As long as you have a prayer life and a bible; you will never feel lonely, rejected and idle in the race of life.

When good friends disconnect from you, let them go, they might have seen something new in a different direction.

Confidence in yourself and in God is the only way to bring you out of captivity

Never train a child to waste his/her time.

The mind is the greatest assets of a great future.

You walk by common sense run by principles and fly by instruction.

Those who fly in flight of life fly alone.

Up in the air you are alone. No one can toll you accept the compass of knowledge and information

I have seen a tolling vehicle I have seen a tolling ship I have never seen a tolling airplane.

I exercise my judgment and make a decision every minute of the day.

Chapter 2 - How to Engage the Enemy in Warfare

Decisions are crucial, critical and vital with reference to your future.

So many people wish for a great future. You can only work towards a great future.

Your celebrity status began when you discovered your talent. What are you good at? Work at it with all commitment.

Prayers will sustain you but the wisdom of God will prosper you.

When I met Oyedepo, his teachings changed my perspective, but

when I met Ibiyeomie; His teaching changed my perception.

I will be successful in ministry if only I concentrate and focus my energy in the work of the ministry.

It took the late Dr. Vincent Pearle Norman's book to open my mind towards kingdom success.

CHAPTER 3
PRAYER OF SALVATION

"Neither is there salvation in any other: for there is none other name under heaven given among men, whereby we must be saved." **Acts4:12**

What must I do to determine my salvation?

To be saved we must be born again! The word says as many as received him, to them gave He power to become the sons of God. Even to them that believe on his name.

To qualify for divine visitation do the following sincerely,

1) Acknowledge that you are a sinner and that he died for you. **Rom3:23.**

2) Repent of your sins. **Acts 3:19, Luke13:5, 2Peter3:9**

3) Believe in your heart that Jesus died for your sin. **Romans10:10**

Chapter 3 - Prayer of Salvation

4) Confess Jesus as the Lord over your life. **Romans10:10, Acts2:21**

Now repeat this Prayer after me

Say Lord Jesus, I accept you today, as my Lord and my savior, forgive me of my sins wash me with your blood. Right now, I believe, I am sanctified, I am save, I am free, I am free from the Power of sin to serve the Lord Jesus. Thank you Lord for saving me. Amen.

Congratulation: YOU ARE NOW A BORN AGAIN CHRISTAIN

AGAIN I SAY TO YOU CONGRATULATION

I adjure you to watch the Spirit of God bear witness with your Spirit confirming His word with signs following. The word says The Spirit itself beareth witness with our spirit, that we are the children of God.

MIRACLE CARE OUTREACH

"...But that the members should have the same care one for another" **1cor12:25**

We are all members of the body of Christ. Jesus commanded us to love our neighbor as ourselves. This includes caring for one another as a member of one body. True love is expressed in caring and giving. The word says for God so Love He gave….

Reach out to someone in need of Jesus, help someone in crisis find Christ. Look out and prove your love to Jesus by caring and inviting your friends and associates to find Jesus the Healer.

Invite your friends to our Home Care Cell Fellowship (Miracle chapel Intl Satellite fellowship) In the USA at 33 Schley Street Newark New Jersey 07112.

If you are in Nigeria—MIRACLE OF GOD MINISTRIES

A.K.A"MIRACLE CHAPEL INTL" Mpama –Egbu-Owerri Imo state Nigeria.

(Home Care Cell fellowship Group).We meet every Tuesday at 6:00pm-7:00pm.

Chapter 3 - Prayer of Salvation

LIFE IS NOT ALL ABOUT DURATION BUT ITS ALL ABOUT DONATION

What does the above statement mean?....

"Life consists not in accumulation of material wealth.." **Luke12:15.**

"But it's all about liberality....meaning- what you can give and share with others." **Proverb11:25.**

When you live for others--You live forever- because you out live your generation by the legacy you live behind after you depart into glory to be with the Lord. But when you live to yourself - you are reduced to self—you are easily forgotten when you die and depart in glory.

Permit me to admonish you today to live your life to be a blessing to a soul connected to you today. I want you to know that so many souls are connected and looking up to you, and through you so many souls will be saved and rescued from destruction. Will you disciple someone today to find Jesus Christ?

"As a genuine Christian; it is your duty to evangelize Jesus Christ to all you meet on your way. Jesus is still in the healing business-Jesus is still doing miracles from time of old to now. Therefore tell someone about Jesus Christ today, disciple and bring them to Church."
John 1:45 Philip findeth Nathanael....

Please to prove the sincerity of your love for God today; please become a soul winner. The dignity of your Christianity is hidden in your boldness to proclaim and evangelize Jesus Christ to all you meet on your way.

There is a question mark on the integrity of your Christianity until you become a life soul winner. Invite someone to join us worship the Lord Jesus this coming Sunday.

Amen

Chapter 3 - Prayer of Salvation

MIRACLE OF GOD MINISTRIES
PILLARS OF THE COMMISSION

We Believe Preach and Practice the following,

1) We believe and preach Salvation to every living human being

2) We believe and preach Repentance and forgiveness of sins

3) We believe and preach the baptism of the Holy Spirit and Spiritual gifts

4) We believe and teach the Prosperity

5) We believe and preach Divine Healing and Miracles (Signs &Wonder)

6) We believe and preach Faith

7) We believe and Proclaim the Power of God (Supernatural)

8) We believe and Proclaim Praise& Worship to God

9) We believe and preach Wisdom

10) We believe and preach Holiness (Consecration)

11) We believe and preach Vision

12) We believe and teach the Word of God

13) We believe and teach Success

14) We believe and practice Prayer

15) We believe and teach Deliverance

This 15 stones form the Pillars of Our Commission.

Become part of this church family and follow this great move of God

MY HEART FELT PRAYER FOR YOU

It is my prayer that you testify today about the goodness of the Lord. I desire for you to have an encounter with our Lord Jesus Christ.

Now let me Pray for you:

Heavenly father may today be a day of new beginning for this precious love one. Lord God of heaven open a new chapter in the life of this precious love one reading this book today.

Chapter 3 - Prayer of Salvation

May all their prayers be answered in the mighty name of Jesus. We thank you Jesus for hearing us. In Jesus mighty name.

Amen.

SOLUTION TO PRAYERS

For the most part, we must make prayer a lifestyle. If our prayer must be answered, then must be armed with what to do, how to do it and when to do it.

It is written *"But thou, when thou prayest, enter into thy closet, and when thou hast shut thy door, pray to thy Father which is in secret; and thy Father which seeth in secret shall reward thee openly. But when ye pray, use not vain repetitions, as the heathen do: for they think that they shall be heard for their much speaking. Be not ye therefore like unto them: for your Father knoweth what things ye have need of, before ye ask him."* **(Mathew6:6-8)**

CHAPTER 4
ABOUT THE AUTHOR

Rev Franklin N Abazie is the founding and Presiding Pastor of Miracle of God Ministries with headquarters in Newark, New Jersey USA and a branch church in Owerri- Imo State Nigeria. He is following the footsteps of one of his mentors, Oral Roberts (Healing Evangelist) of the blessed memory.

The Lord passed Oral Roberts healing mantle two days before he went to be with the Lord at age 91 into the hand of healing evangelist-Rev Franklin N Abazie in a vision.

In all his services the Power and Presence of God is present to heal all in his audience. He is an ordained man of God with a Healing Ministry reviving the healing and miracle ministry of Jesus Christ of Nazareth.

Chapter 4 - About the Author

Pastor Franklin N Abazie, is called by God with a unique mandate:

"THE MOMENT IS DUE TO IMPACT YOUR WORLD THROUGH THE REVIVAL OF THE HEALING & MIRACLE MINISTRY OF JESUS CHRIST OF NAZARETH
I AM SENDING YOU TO RESTORE HEALTH UNTO THEE AND I WILL HEAL THEE OF THY WOUNDS. SAID THE LORD OF HOST"

He is a gifted ardent Teacher of the word of God who operates also in the office of a Prophet, generating and attracting undeniable signs & wonders, special miracles and healings, with apostolic fireworks of the Holy Ghost.

He is the founding and presiding senior Pastor of this fast growing Healing ministry.

BOOKS BY REV FRANKLIN N ABAZIE

1) Commanding Abundance
2) The outcome of faith
3) Understanding the secret of prevailing prayers
4) Understanding the secret of the man God uses
5) Activating my due Season
6) Overcoming Divine Verdicts
7) The Outcome of Divine Wisdom
8) Understanding God's Restoration Mandate
9) Walking in the Victory and Authority of the truth
10) Gods Covenant Exemption
11) Destiny Restoration Pillars
12) Provoking Acceptable Praise
13) Understanding Divine Judgment
14) Activating Angelic Re-enforcement
15) Provoking Un-Merited Favor
16) The Benefits of the Speaking faith
17) Understanding Divine Arrangement

18) Understanding Divine Healing
19) The Mystery of Endurance
20) Obeying Divine Instructions
21) Understanding the Voice of God
22) Never give up on Hope
23) The prevailing Power of faith
24) Understanding Divine Prosperity
25) The Reward of Prayer
26) Covenant Keys to Answered Prayers
27) Activating the Forces of Vengeance
28) Put your faith to work
29) Where is your trust?
30) The Audacity of the Blood of Jesus
31) Redeeming Your Days
32) The force of Vision
33) Breaking the shackles of Family Curses
34) Wisdom for Marriage Stability
35) The winners Faith
36) The Prayer solution
37) The power of Prayer
38) Prayer strategy
39) The prayer that works
40) Walking in Forgiveness
41) The power of the grace of God

42) The power of Persistence
43) Overcoming Divine verdicts
44) The audacity of the blood of Jesus.
45) The prevailing power of the blood of Jesus
46) The benefit of the speaking faith.
47) Fearless faith
48) Redeeming Your Days.
49) The Supernatural Power of Prophecy
50) The companionship of the Holy Spirit
51) Understanding Divine Judgement
52) Understanding Divine Prosperity
53) Dominating Controlling Forces
54) The winners Faith
55) Destiny Restoration Pillars
56) Developing Spiritual Muscles
57) Inexplicable faith
58) The lifestyle of Prayer
59) Developing a positive attitude in life.
60) The mystery of Divine supply
61) Encounter with God's Power
62) Walking in love
63) Praying in the Spirit
64) How to provoke your testimony

65) Walking in the reality of the Anointing
66) The reality of new birth
67) The price of freedom
68) The Supernatural power of faith
69) The Power of Persistence
70) The intellectual components of Redemption
71) Overcoming Fear
72) The Force of Vision
73) Overcoming Prevailing Challenges
74) The Power of the Grace of God
75) My life & Ministry
76) The Mystery of Praise

MIRACLE OF GOD MINISTRIES

NIGERIA CRUSADE 2012

MIRACLE OF GOD MINISTRIES
NIGERIA CRUSADE 2012

MIRACLE OF GOD MINISTRIES

NIGERIA CRUSADE

2012

MIRACLE OF GOD MINISTRIES

NIGERIA CRUSADE

2012

www.ingramcontent.com/pod-product-compliance
Lightning Source LLC
Chambersburg PA
CBHW021448080526
44588CB00009B/747